THE BOOK OF

TAPPING & CLAPPING

Wonderful songs and rhymes passed down from generation to generation

Compiled by John M. Feierabend

GIA FIRST STEPS • CHICAGO

Compiled by
John M. Feierabend

Artwork: Diana Appleton
Design: Nina Fox

GIA First Steps is an imprint of
GIA Publications, Inc.

ISBN: 1-57999-054-1
G-4977

Library of Congress Cataloging-in-Publication Data

The Book of Tapping & Clapping: wonderful songs and rhymes passed down from generation to generation / compiled by John M. Feierabend.

     p. cm. – (*First Steps in Music*)

    Chiefly in English; includes a few selections in French, German, Italian, Polish, and Spanish, with English translation. Includes index.

    Summary: A collection of songs and rhymes that involve finger play, for infants and toddlers.

    ISBN 1-57999-054-1 (pbk.)

    1) Nursery rhymes. 2) Children's poetry. 3) Children's songs – Texts. [1. Nursery rhymes. 2. Songs. 3. Finger play.] I) Title: Tapping & Clapping. II) Title: Book of Tapping and Clapping. III) Title: Tapping and Clapping. IV) Feierabend, John Martin. V) Series.

PZ8.3 .B64455 1999
[E] – dc21   99-047221

Once upon a time, parents (and grandparents) soothed and amused their babies with songs that were sung to them when they were children. As those babies grew up and became parents, they would sing those same tunes to their children. In this way, wonderful songs and rhymes would be passed orally, linking one generation to another through shared memories of comfort and joy.

Today, families are more rushed for time than ever before, and extended families are much less common than they once were. Because of this, cherished songs and rhymes, many of them hundreds of years old, are gradually being forgotten. Our genuine traditional music is in danger of being supplanted by market-driven ear candy, tunes that may provide a temporary rush but exist mostly to help sell this year's hot new toys.

The *First Steps in Music* series of books and recordings is an attempt to preserve the rich repertoire of traditional and folk literature; to enable today's families to remember and to learn songs and rhymes that have inspired wonder and joy in children for generations.

The songs and rhymes contained in this book have been gathered over the past twenty years. Many of the most interesting examples were collected from the elderly who often recalled songs and/or rhymes with great affection, reminding them of loving moments they had shared with young people in the past.

Tapping on the bottom of baby's foot and gently touching the parts of baby's face, fingers, or legs are natural games that have brought joy to children for generations. Clapping baby's hands together or inviting baby to clap onto your hands lets baby and adult communicate through play without words.

It is my hope that the collections of songs and rhymes presented in this series will help parents and other loving adults comfort and inspire wonder in children, for generations to come.

John M. Feierabend

How to Tap

Tapping on the bottom of baby's feet is as playful and developmentally appropriate in newborn children as it is during their next few years. Tap on the bottom of baby's feet, keeping beat while chanting a rhyme or singing a song. Other rhymes invite gentle tapping on the face or other parts of the body. As baby develops, invite baby to tap on the bottom of your feet or his

tap the foot

tap the nose

have the child tap

or her own feet while you chant or sing following the speed of baby's tapping.

About Tapping

Not too long ago, much baby play centered around playing with baby's feet, such as tapping on the bottom of baby's feet while pretending to put on horseshoes or repair worn-out shoes. Sometimes the tapping represented a flea climbing up from toes to head and back again. Sometimes baby's face was gently tapped while naming various persons or objects. Tapping encourages a feeling for the beat in rhymes and songs while entertaining baby with imaginative play.

TAPPING

The Lord Mayor and His Men

Here sits the Lord Mayor,

tap baby's forehead

Here sit his men.

tap near each of baby's eyes

Here sits the rooster

tap on one of baby's cheekbones

And here sits the hen.

tap on the other cheekbone

Here sit the chickens

tap on baby's nose

And here they run in.

tap on baby's mouth

Chin chopper, chin chopper, chin chopper, chin.

gently hold baby's chin and shake up and down

Adam and Eve

Adam and Eve went up my sleeve
To fetch me down some candy.
Adam and Eve came down my sleeve
And said there was none 'til Monday.

with one finger, tap the beat going up baby's arm, then down his/her arm

Hickory, Dickory, Dock

Hickory, Dickory, Dock,

with two fingers, walk up baby's arm

The mouse ran up the clock.
The clock struck one

kiss baby's forehead

And down he run.

with two fingers, walk down baby's arm

Hickory, Dickory, Dock.

Akron Beacon

(There were once two newspapers in Akron, the Akron Beacon Journal and the Times Press.)

Akron

tap forehead

Beacon

tap chin

Journal

tap right cheek

Times

tap left cheek

Press

press baby's nose

Climb Up the Ladder

Climb up the ladder,

with two fingers, walk up baby's arm

Hurry to the slide.
Sit at the top
And down you slide.

slide fingers down baby's arm

Johnny, Johnny, Whoops

Johnny, Johnny, Johnny, Johnny,
Whoops! Johnny,
Johnny, Whoops!
Johnny, Johnny, Johnny, Johnny.

starting with the little finger of one of baby's hands, say "Johnny" as you tap each of baby's fingers; slide your finger down baby's index finger and up toward the thumb as you say, "Whoops!," then reverse the order as you move to the other hand and start with the thumb, saying "Johnny, Whoops, Johnny, Johnny, Johnny, Johnny"

Mix a Pancake

Mix a pancake, stir a pancake,

draw a circle in baby's palm

Pop it in the pan.

tap once onto baby's palm and close his/her hand

Fry a pancake, toss a pancake,

tap the beat up onto baby's fist, bouncing baby's fist, ending with one strong tap

Catch it if you can!

pull baby's fist to your mouth and pretend to nibble

Little Hand

Pat it, kiss it,

stroke hand once and kiss it

Stroke it, bless it.

continue stroking baby's hand

Three days sunshine, three days rain,
Little hand's all well again.

Pumpkins

One little pumpkin,

with one finger from each hand, walk up baby from toe to head

Climbing through the pumpkin patch,
He went up to the witch's house.

A medium-sized pumpkin,

with the tips of all your fingers, walk up baby from toe to head

Climbing through the pumpkin patch,
He went up to the witch's house.

A great big pumpkin,

with whole hands, walk up baby from toe to head

Climbing through the pumpkin patch,
He went up to the witch's house.

Rub a Dub Dub

Rub a dub dub,

perform motions as if drying baby's hair with a towel

Three men in the tub
And who do you think they be?
The butcher, the baker,
The candlestick maker;
Turn them out, knaves all three.

My Mother and Your Mother

My mother and your mother

gently tug on baby's nose

Went over the way.

Said my mother to your mother,

with the other hand, pretend to chop off baby's

nose

"It's a chop a nose day!"

There Was a Little Man

There was a little man

waggle finger at baby

And he had a little crumb,

tickle corner of baby's mouth

And over the mountain he did run.

run two fingers up baby's arm, over baby's

head, and down the other arm

With a belly full of fat,

pat baby's belly

And a big tall hat,

pat baby's head

And a pancake stuck to his bum,
bum, bum.

pat baby's behind or tap on the beat starting on

baby's head, down to his/her feet

One, Two, Three

One, two, three,

tap on baby's knee

Tickle your knee.

tickle baby's knee

Four, five, six,

tap on baby's tummy

Pick up sticks.

tickle baby's tummy

Seven, eight, nine,

tap on baby's chin

You're all mine!

hug baby

Pizza, Pickle, Pumpernickel

Pizza, pickle, pumpernickel,

bounce baby on knee

My little guy shall have a tickle.

One for his nose,

tap twice on baby's nose

One for his toes

tap twice on baby's toes

And one for his tummy where the
hot dog goes.

draw a circle on baby's tummy and end with a

tickle

Pitter, Patter

Pit-ter, pat-ter, pit-ter, pat-ter, Lis-ten to the rain.

Pit-ter, pat-ter, pit-ter, pat-ter, On my win-dow pane.

Verse

Pitter, patter, pitter, patter,
Listen to the rain.

*alternating hands, tap the beat on some part of
baby's body*

Pitter, patter, pitter, patter,
On my window pane.

*on each repetition, tap on some other part of
baby's body*

So Many Shoes...

Is Johnny In?

Is Johnny in?

tap on the bottom of baby's foot

Yes he is!
Can he mend a shoe?
Yes, one or two.
Here's a nail,
There's a nail,
Tick, tack, too.

Variation

Is Master Smith within?

tap on the bottom of baby's foot

Yes, that he is.
Can he set a shoe?
Aye, narry, two.
Here a nail and there a nail,
Tick, tack, too.

Fire, Water, Earth and Air

(a riddle about the blacksmith)
A shoemaker makes shoes without
   any leather,
With all the four elements put
   together.
Fire, Water, Earth and Air,
And every customer takes two pair.

Cobbler, Cobbler

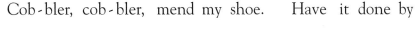

Cob-bler, cob-bler, mend my shoe. Have it done by

half - past two. Tu - ra - lu - ra - lu.

Half - past two is much too late, Have it done by

half - past eight. Tu - ra - lu - ra - lu.

Verse

Cobbler, cobbler, mend my shoe.
Have it done by half-past two.
Tu-ra-lu-ra-lu.

Half-past two is much too late,
Have it done by half-past eight.
Tu-ra-lu-ra-lu.

Cock-a-Doodle Doo

Cock - a - dood - le   doo,   My dame has lost her

shoe.   My   mas - ter's   lost   his

fid - dling stick And   doesn't know what to   do.

Verse 1

Cock-a-doodle doo,

tap on the bottom of one of baby's feet

My dame has lost her shoe.
My master's lost his fiddling stick
And doesn't know what to do.

Verse 2

Cock-a-doodle doo,

tap on the bottom of the other foot

What is my Dame to do?

'Til Master finds his fiddling stick
She'll dance without a shoe.

Verse 3

Cock-a-doodle doo,

tap on the bottom of both feet

My dame has found her shoe.
And Master's found his fiddling
  stick,
Sing doodle, doodle, doo.

Hob, Shoe, Hob

Hob, shoe, hob,

tap on the bottom of baby's foot

Hob, shoe, hob,
Here a nail and there a nail,
And that's well shod.

The Man in the Mune

(a Scottish tapping)
The man in the mune
Is making shune.
Tuppence a pair an'
They're a' dune.

tap on the bottom of baby's foot

Robert Barnes

Robert Barnes, fellow fine,
Can you shoe this horse of mine?
Yes, good sir, that I can
As well as any other man.
Here's a nail, there's a prod.
Now, good sir, your horse is shod.

Variation 1

Jack Smith of Munterlony,
Tell me, can you shoe this pony?
Yes indeed for that I can
As well as any other man.
Here's a nail, there's a prod,
Now, good sir, your horse is shod.

Variation 2

John Smith, fellow fine,
Can you shoe this horse of mine?
Yes I can and that I can
As well as any other man.
Put a nail upon his toe,
That's to make him trot and go.
Put a nail upon his sole,
That's to make him pay the toll.
Put a nail upon his heel,
That's to make him pace weel,
Pace weel, pace weel.

Variation 3

Blacksmith very fine,
Can you shoe this horse of mine
So that it can cut a shine?
Yes, master, that I can,
As well as any other man.
Bring the mare before the stall,
One nail drives it all.
Whip Jack, Spur Tom,
Blow the bellows good old man.

Shoe the Horse

Shoe a little horse,
Shoe a little mare,
But let the little colt go
Bare, bare, bare.

Variation 1

Shoe the colt,
Shoe the wild mare.
Here a nail,
There a nail,
Yet she goes bare!

Variation 2

Shoe a little horse,
Shoe a little mare
With a tap, tap here
And a tap, tap there.
But let the little colt go bare,
  bare, bare.

Variation 3

Shoe the old horse
  tap on the bottom of baby's foot
Shoe the old mare.
Pound a nail here,
Pound a nail there,
But let the little colty foot
  go bare, bare, bare.
  gently rub the bottom of baby's foot

Variation 4

Shoe the pony, shoe,
Shoe the wild mare.
Put a sack upon her back
And see if she will bear!

Variation 5

Pitty, patty, polt,
  tap on the bottom of baby's foot
Shoe a little colt.
Here a nail, there a nail,
Pitty, patty, polt.

Down the Street

There's a cobbler down the street
  tap on the bottom of baby's foot
Mending shoes for little feet;
With a bang and a bang
And a bang, bang, bang;
With a bang and a bang
And a bang, bang, bang.

Mending shoes the whole day long,
Mending shoes to make them strong;
With a bang and a bang
And a bang, bang, bang;
With a bang and a bang
And a bang, bang, bang.

Cobbler Makes Shoes

The cobbler, the cobbler, makes
  my shoes;
He pounds them rap, rap, rap!
He makes them small, he makes
  them big,
And ever he pounds, tap, tap!

Head, Shoulders, Knees and Toes...

Here Are Baby's Eyes

Here are baby's eyes so bright,
Always sparkling, full of light.
Here is baby's little nose,
Here's his/her mouth so like a rose.
Here are teeth all shining bright;
Be careful, baby, what they bite.

Here are two pink, little ears,
Oh, how many things he/she hears.
Here are cheeks so soft and sweet,
Look like they were made to eat.
The forehead's where wee faces
  begin;
Here's the end—a dimpled chin.

*tap on each part of baby's face as
mentioned*

Boo Heady

Boo heady,
tap on baby's forehead
Boo heady,
Boo heady,
BOO!
a gentle tickle on baby's tummy

Baby's Fingers

These are <u>baby's</u> fingers,
tap on baby's body parts as mentioned
substitute baby's name
These are baby's toes.
This is baby's belly button,
'Round and 'round it goes.
tickle baby's tummy

Two Little Eyes

Two little eyes to look around,

tap near baby's eyes

Two little ears to hear each sound,

tap on baby's ears

One little nose to smell what's sweet,

tap on baby's nose

One little mouth that likes to eat.

tap on baby's mouth

Head and Shoulders

Head and shoulders baby one, two,
   three,
Head and shoulders baby one, two,
   three,
Head and shoulders, head and shoulders,
Head and shoulders baby one, two,
   three.

"head"-touch baby's head

"shoulders"-touch baby's shoulders

"baby"-give baby a little hug

tap baby's legs and clap your hands three times

   on "one, two, three"

substitute other body parts such as "knees and

   ankles, baby"

Ten Little Fingers, Ten Little Toes

Ten little fingers,

tap on each body part as it is mentioned

Ten little toes.
Two little eyes
And one little nose.
Two little cheeks
And one little chin.
One little mouth where the taffy goes
   in!

Brow Bender, Eye Peeper

Brow Bender,
Eye Peeper,
Nose Smeller,
Mouth Eater,
Chin Chopper,
Knock at the door,

gently knock on baby's forehead

Peep in,

raise baby's eyebrow

Lift the latch,

gently lift baby's nose

Walk in.

with one finger, wiggle baby's lips

Variation 1

Brow Binker,

tap parts of baby's face as mentioned

Eye Winker,
Cheek Cherry,
Mouth Merry,
Nose Noppy,
Chin Choppy.
Gully, gully, gully.

tickle under baby's chin

Variation 2

Brow Brinky, Eye Winky,

gently tap on baby's forehead then near eye

Chin Choppy, Nose Noppy,

gently tap on baby's chin then on nose

Cheek Cherry, Mouth Merry.

gently tap on baby's cheek then mouth

Mmm, Mmm, Mmm!

draw a circle on baby's tummy

Variation 3

Head Bumper,
Eye Winker,
Nose Dropper,
Mouth Eater,
Chin Chopper.
Gully, gully, gully!
or Billy, Billy, Billy, Billy, Boo!

tickle under baby's chin

Variation 4

Here's where the coachman sits,

tap baby's forehead

Here's where he lost his whip.

tap the bridge of baby's nose

Eye Winker,
Tom Tinker,
Nose Dropper,
Mouth Eater,
Chin Chopper, Chin Chopper, Chin
  Chopper, Chin.

Variation 5

Louse Head,

touch baby's hair

Fore Head,

touch baby's forehead

Eye Winker,

tap near one eye

Tom Tinker,

tap near the other eye

Nose Dropper,
Mouth Eater,

touch baby's mouth

Chin Chopper,

touch baby's chin

Get ya, get ya.

tickle under baby's chin

Variation 6

Eye Winker,
Tom Tinker,
Nose Smeller,
Mouth Eater,
Chin Chopper,
Chin Chopper.

Variation 7

Tae Titly,
Little Fitty,
Shin Sharpy,
Knee Knapy,
Hinchie Pinchy,

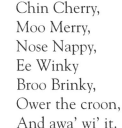

Wymie Bulgy,
Breast Berry,
Chin Cherry,
Moo Merry,
Nose Nappy,
Ee Winky
Broo Brinky,
Ower the croon,
And awa' wi' it.

tap on baby from toe to head

Variation 8

Toe Tickley,

pat on baby's body parts from toe to head as

mentioned

Little Footy,
Shin Sharpy,
Knee Cappy,
Hinchie Pinchie,
Wimie Bulgy,
Breast Berry,
Chin Cherry,
Mouth Merry,
Nose Nappy,
Eye Winky,
Brow Brinky,
Over the crown
And away we go.

Variation 9

Toe Titty,

tap on baby from toe to head

Wee Footy,
Shin Chappy,
Knee Nappy,
Hinchie Pinchie,
Wymie Bulgy,
Breast Berry,
Neck Nappy,
Eye Winkie,
Brow Blinkie,
Over the crown,
Down we go,

run fingers down baby from head to toe

Down we go,
Down we go.

Wash Hands, Wash

Wash hands, wash.

stroke baby's hands on the beat

The men have gone to plough.
If you want to wash your hands,
Wash your hands, now.

try other motions such as, comb hair, comb;

wash cheeks, wash; etc...

Toe Town

'Tis all the way to toe town

walk with fingers from baby's knee to toes

Beyond the knee hill,
That <u>baby</u> goes to watch

substitute baby's name

The soldiers drill.
There's one, two, three,
Four and five in a row.

tap on each toe

A captain and his men

hold all of baby's toes at once and wiggle them

And on the other side you know,
Are six, seven, eight, nine, ten.

tap on each toe

 # Marks the Spot!

Going on a Treasure Hunt

Going on a treasure hunt,

draw a wavy line on baby's back

"X" marks the spot.

draw an "X" on baby's back

Around in a circle,

draw a circle

And a plop, plop, plop.

touch three points of a triangle

Chills go down,

draw a line going down

And chills go up,

draw a line going up

And chills go all around.

draw a wavy line all around baby's back

Crack the egg,

tap on baby's head

Feel the breeze,

blow on baby's neck

And squeeze.

pinch a small amount of skin on the spine

"X" Marks the Spot

"X" marks the spot;

draw a large "X" on baby's back

Dot, dot, dot.

draw three dots on baby's back, one on each shoulder and one at the bottom of baby's back

Up and down,

with one finger, draw up and down baby's back

'Round and 'round,

draw circles on baby's back

Ooooooooooo.

gently tickle from bottom to top of baby's back

Variation

"X" marks the spot,
Dot, dot, dot.
Three lines down,
A circle around,
A pinch, a squeeze,
A soft wind blows.
Gotcha!

tickle baby

Criss-Cross, Applesauce

Criss-cross, applesauce.

draw a large "X" on baby's back, with a dot in the center

Spiders crawling up your spine.

gently tickle from the bottom to the top of baby's back

Cool breeze,

gently blow on the back of baby's neck

Tight squeeze,

gently press down on baby's shoulders

Now you've got the chillies.

gently tickle from the top to the bottom of baby's back

Looking for Treasure

Looking for a treasure, looking for a treasure,

draw two figure eights on baby's back

"X" marks the spot,

draw an "X" on baby's back

"X" marks the spot.

draw another "X"

Two dots,

touch baby's back twice

A line,

draw a line down the spine

A breeze,

blow on baby's neck

A squeeze.

gently pinch baby's neck

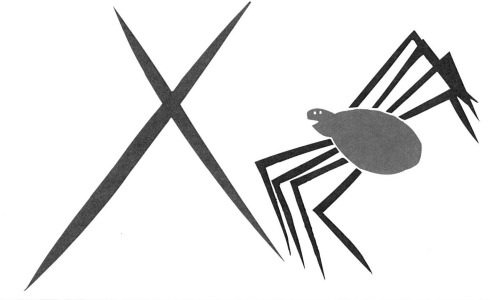

Animal Friends

Kommt Ein Bär (Here Comes a Bear)

German

Kommt ein Bär, der tappt so schwer;
walk with fingers up one of baby's legs
Kommt ein Mäuschen, baut sich ein Häuschen.
walk with fingers up the other leg
Kommt ein Mückchen, baut ein Brückchen;
walk fingers up one of baby's arms
Kommt ein Floh, der macht so.
walk fingers up the other arm and then tickle

Translation:

Here comes a bear, he pads along heavily
Here comes a mouse, he builds a house.
Here comes a mosquito, he builds a bridge:
Here comes a flea, he goes like this.

Mousie, Mousie

Here comes a mousie, mousie

with one finger, tap on the beat from baby's palm to baby's shoulder

Looking for a housie, housie.
Knock at the door,

gently tap on baby's forehead

Peep in.

with one finger, gently lift baby's eyebrow

Lift the latch

with one finger gently lift baby's nose

And walk in.

with two fingers, walk up baby's chin to his/her mouth

Diddlety, Diddlety, Dumpty

Diddlety, Diddlety, Dumpty!

bounce baby on your knee

The cat ran up the plum tree.

walk two fingers up baby's arm

It took half the town to bring her back down,

walk two fingers down baby's other arm

Diddlety, Diddlety, Dumpty!

bounce baby again

There Was a Mouse

There was a mouse,
For want of stairs,

walk up baby's arm with two fingers

Went down a rope

slide two fingers down baby's other arm

To say his prayers.

hold baby's hands and put them together

Creepy Mouse

Creepy mouse, creepy mouse;

with two fingers, walk up baby's leg

And along came a big black cat.

with two heavy hands, walk up baby's legs

SCAT!

clap your hands once

On My Toe There Is a Flea

On my toe there is a flea, Now he's climb-ing up on me.

Past my tum-my, past my nose, On my head where my hair grows.

On my head there is a flea, Now he's climb-ing down on me.

Past my tum-my, past my knee, On my toe, take that you flea!

Verse

On my toe there is a flea,

tap on baby from toe to head

Now he's climbing up on me.
Past my tummy, past my nose,
On my head where my hair grows.

On my head there is a flea,

tap on baby from head to toe

Now he's climbing down on me.
Past my tummy, past my knee,
On my toe, take that you flea!

tickle the bottom of baby's foot

Here Goes a Turtle

Here goes a turtle up the hill,
Creepy, creepy, creepy, creepy.

walk fingers from baby's palm to shoulder

Here goes a rabbit up the hill,
Boing, boing, boing, boing.
Here goes an elephant up the hill,
Thud, thud, thud, thud.
Here goes a snake up the hill,
Slither, slither, slither, slither.
Here comes a rock down the hill,

set your fist on baby's shoulder

Boom, boom, boom, boom, CRASH!

*slide down baby's arm and place your fist in
baby's palm*

Una Vieja Piza un Gato (The Old Woman and the Cat) *Spanish*

Una vieja piza un gato,
Con la punto de zapato.
Pobre vieja, pobre gato,
Pobre punta de zapato.

Translation:

The old woman stepped on a cat
With the toe of her shoe.
Poor old woman, poor cat,
Poor toe of the shoe.

Soft Kitty

Soft kitty, warm kitty,

stroke top of baby's hand

Little ball of fur;

make baby's hand into a fist

Lazy kitty, pretty kitty,

stroke baby's hand again

Purr, purr, purr.

stroke under baby's chin

This Is the Rooster

This is the little rooster,

tap on baby's forehead

This is the little hen.

tap on baby's chin

This is the baby Pullet.

tap on baby's nose

This is the little _____

*tap on baby's forehead and let him/her fill in
the word "Rooster"*

This is the little_____

*tap on baby's chin and let him/her fill in the
word "Hen"*

This is the baby_____

*tap on baby's nose and let him/her fill in the
word "Pullet"; when he/she says
"Pullet", gently pull baby's nose*

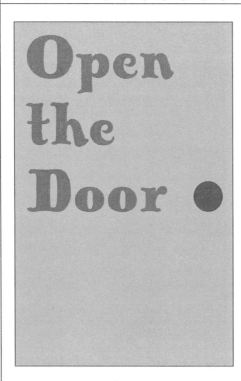

Knock at the Door

Knock at the door,

gently tap on baby's forehead

Peep in,

raise baby's eyelid slightly

Lift the latch,

with one finger lift baby's nose

Walk in.

wiggle fingers on baby's lips

Go way down cellar and eat apples.

tickle baby's neck

Variation 1

Knock at the door,

gently tap baby's forehead

Peek in,

raise one of baby's eyebrows

Lift the latch

with one finger, lift baby's nose

And walk in.

wiggle fingers on baby's lips

Take a chair,

touch baby's tooth

Leave it there.

take finger away

Slam the door behind you.

cover baby's mouth with your hand

Knock, Knock

Knock, knock,

gently tap on baby's forehead

Peek in,

raise baby's eyelid slightly

Open the latch

with one finger, lift baby's nose

And walk right in.

wiggle fingers on baby's lips

How do you do,

hold baby's chin and shake up and down

Mister Chinny Chin, Chin?

Variation 2

Knock   at   the   door!   Peek   in!

Pull   the   latch   And   walk   in!

Verse

Knock at the door!

tap forehead with fist

Peek in!

raise eyelid slightly

Pull the latch

lift the tip of nose

And walk in!

walk two fingers up chin and into mouth

Variation 3

Ring the bell,

gently tug on baby's hair

Knock at the door,

tap on baby's forehead

Draw the latch

with one finger, lift baby's nose

And walk in.

with one finger, wiggle baby's lips

Variation 4

Ring the bell,

tug a little of baby's hair

Knock at the door,

gently knock on baby's forehead

Lift the latch

gently lift baby's nose

And walk in.

with one finger, wiggle baby's lips

the book of tapping & clapping

How to Clap

Children nine months old and younger enjoy having you hold onto their hands and clap them together in time with a song or rhyme. As baby nears twelve months, have baby rest his or her palms on top of your palms. Tap up onto baby's palms while singing the song or reciting the rhyme. After a short while, share the songs and rhymes with baby's hands resting on

clap baby's palms

clap separately

clap together

top of yours. Soon baby will tap onto your hands. Speak the rhyme or sing the song while baby claps. Stop when baby stops. Sing or speak following the speed of baby's clapping. You are sure to see smiles as baby learns he or she can "control" the song or rhyme by clapping onto your hands.

About Clapping

For many generations, playing "Pat-a-Cake" with baby's hands has been one of the principal joys of adult-child play. But there are other songs and rhymes meant for clapping games with baby. The wonderful, imaginative play involved in these hand-clapping games continues to provide opportunities for adults and children to communicate through smiles and laughter long before baby can communicate his or her feelings in words. In addition, these songs and rhymes enable baby to acquire an innate sense of the beat in music.

CLAPPING

Clap Your Hands

Baby, baby, clap your hands!
Where London's built, there London
　stands;
And there's a bed in London Town
On which my baby shall lie down.

Tape Petites Mains
(Clap Little Hands) *French*

Tape, tape petites mains,
clap baby's hands
Tourne, tourne petit moulin.
roll baby's hands one over the other

Translation:

Clap, clap little hands,
Turn, turn little wheel.

Andrew Brown

Clap   your hands lit-tle An-drew.   Clap   your hands lit-tle

An-drew Brown.   Clap   your hands   lit-tle   An-drew,

Clap your hands   An   -   drew   Brown.

Verse

Clap your hands little Andrew,
Clap your hands little Andrew Brown.
Clap your hands little Andrew,
Clap your hands Andrew Brown.

Koci, Koci, łapci *Polish*

Ko - ci, ko - ci łap - ci, Po - jed - ziem do bab - ci.

Od bab - ci do cio - ci? Ko - ci, ko - ci, ko - ci.

Verse

Koci, koci łapci,
Pojedziem do babci.
Od babci do cioci?
Koci, koci, koci.

General Translation:

Tickle, tickle fingers,
Going to see Grammy.
Then we'll go see Auntie,
Tickle, tickle, tickle

Miss Mary Mack

Miss Mar - y   Mack,   Mack,   Mack

All   dressed   in   black,   black,   black.

Verse

Miss Mary Mack, Mack, Mack
All dressed in black, black, black.

With silver buttons, buttons, buttons
All down her back, back, back.

She asked her mother, mother, mother
For fifty cents, cents, cents.

To see the elephant, elephant, elephant
Jump over the fence, fence, fence.

He jumped so high, high, high
He touched the sky, sky, sky.

And he didn't come back, back, back
'Til the fourth of July, ly, ly.

Here Comes Daddy

Bring Daddy Home

Bring Daddy home
With a fiddle and a drum,
A pocket full of spices,
An apple and a plum.

Daddy Comes with Cake and Plums

Clap hands, Daddy comes
With a pocket full of plums
And a cake for baby.

Clap, Clap, Handies

Clap, clap, handies,
Mommy's wee born.
Clap, clap, handies,
Daddy's coming home.
Home to his bonnie wee lassie (laddie),
Clap, clap, handies.

Clap Handy

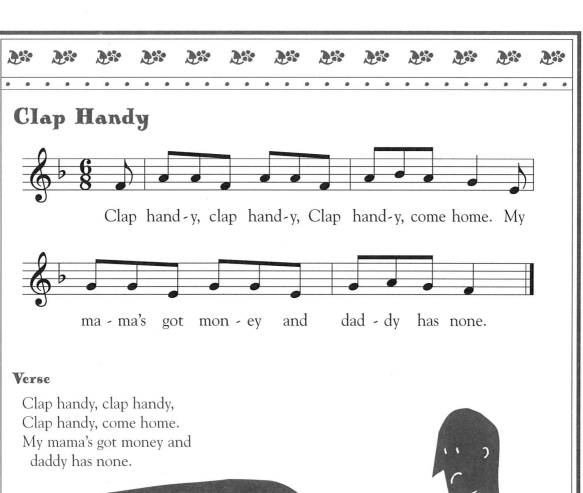

Clap hand-y, clap hand-y, Clap hand-y, come home. My

ma - ma's got mon - ey and dad - dy has none.

Verse

Clap handy, clap handy,
Clap handy, come home.
My mama's got money and
   daddy has none.

Clap Hands 'Til Daddy Comes Home

Clap   hands,   clap hands,   'til   Dad-dy comes home, With

buns   in   his   pock-et   for   ba-by   a-lone.   Clap

hands,   clap hands,   'til   Dad-dy   comes home,   For

Dad-dy   has   mon-ey   and   Mam-my   has   none.

Verse

Clap hands, clap hands, 'til Daddy
   comes home,
With buns in his pocket for <u>baby</u>
   alone.

substitute baby's name

Clap hands, clap hands, 'til Daddy
   comes home,
For Daddy has money and Mammy
   has none.

Qué Linda Manita *Spanish*

Qué   lin - da ma - ni - ta que tie - ne el be - bé!   Qué

lin - da, qué   be - lla, qué crez - cá   o - tra vez.

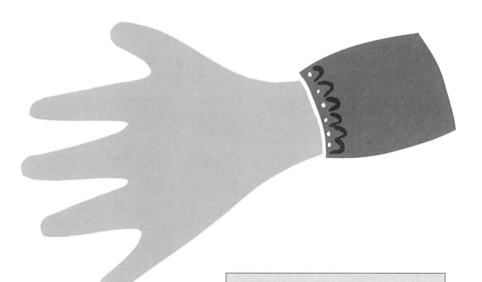

Verse

Qué linda manita que tiene
   el bebé!
Qué linda, qué bella, qué
   crezcá otra vez.

General Translation:

How pretty is the baby's
   little hand.
How pretty, how beautiful,
   how it will grow someday.

Sweets and Other Good Things to Eat

Eier und Salz (Eggs and Salt) *German*

Eier und Salz,
Butter und Schmalz,
Milch und Mehl.
Saffren macht den Kuchen gel.
Schieb, schieb in Ofen rein.

*hold baby's hands and gently push them
toward baby*

Wird er bald gebacken sein.

*pull baby's hands toward your mouth and
nibble on baby's fingers*

Translation:

Eggs and salt,
Butter and lard,
Milk and flour.
Saffron will make the cake yellow.
Put it in the oven.
Soon it will be ready.

Batti Le Manine (Clap Your Little Hands) *Italian*

Bat - ti le ma - ni - ne, A -
Clap your lit - tle hands,

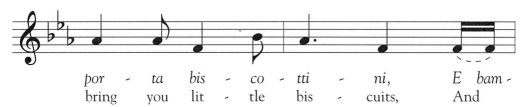

des - so vie - ne pa - pá. Ti
Soon comes your pa - pa. He'll

por - ta bis - co - tti - ni, E bam -
bring you lit - tle bis - cuits, And

bi - no li man - ge - rá.
ba - by will eat them all.

Verse

Batti le manine,
Adesso viene papá.
Ti porta biscottini,
E bambino li mangerá.

Translation:

Clap your little hands,
Soon comes your papa.
He'll bring you little biscuits,
And baby will eat them all.

Backe, Backe, Kuchen *German*

Bac - ke, bac - ke, Kuch - en. Der

bäc - ker hat ger - u - fen.

Wer will gu - ten Kuch - en back - en?

Der muss ha - ben sie - ben sach - en?

Verse

Backe, backe, Kuchen.
Der bäcker hat gerufen.
Wer will guten Kuchen backen?
Der muss haben sieben sachen?

General Translation:

Bake the cake.
The baker is calling.
Who will bake a good cake?
Who has seven good things?

Hot Cross Buns

Hot cross buns, Hot cross buns.

One a pen-ny, two a pen-ny, Hot cross buns.

Verse

Hot cross buns,
Hot cross buns.
One a penny, two a penny,
Hot cross buns.

If you have no daughters,
Give them to your sons.
One a penny, two a penny,
Hot cross buns.

Pat-a-Cake

Pat-a-cake, pat-a-cake, baker's man,
Roll 'em over, roll 'em over, fast as
  you can.
Pat-a-cake, pat-a-cake, baker's man,
Roll 'em over, roll 'em over, throw
  'em in the pan.

Variation

Patty cake, patty cake, baker's man,

clap baby's hands together

Bake me a cake as fast as you can.
Roll it and pat it and mark it with
  a "B,"

move baby's hands in a circle, pat them

together, and write a "B" on them

And put it in the oven for baby and
me!

push baby's hands toward baby, pull them

toward your mouth, and pretend to nibble on

baby's hands

One Potato, Two Potato

One potato, two potato,
Three potato, four;
Five potato, six potato,
Seven potato, more.

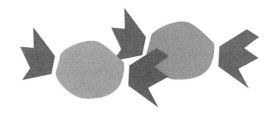

Handy Pandy

Handy Pandy,
Sugar Candy,
Which one will you choose?
Top or bottom?

hide a small object in one hand, then pound

fists together one on top of the other; at the

end, ask the child to guess which hand has the

object

Peas Porridge Hot

Peas porridge hot,
Peas porridge cold,
Peas porridge in the pot
Nine days old.

Some like it hot,
Some like it cold,
Some like it in the pot
Nine days old.

My mammy likes it hot,
My daddy likes it cold,
But I like it in the pot
Nine days old.

Clap for the Animals...

Higglety Pigglety Pop

Higglety Pigglety Pop!
clap hands
The dog has eaten the mop.
The pig's in a hurry,
roll hands
The cat's in a flurry,
Higglety Pigglety Pop!
clap hands

Pit, Pat, Well a Day

Pit, pat, well a day,
clap baby's hands together
Little Robin flew away.
Where can little Robin be?
lift baby's arms
Gone into the cherry tree.
tickle under baby's arm

Index